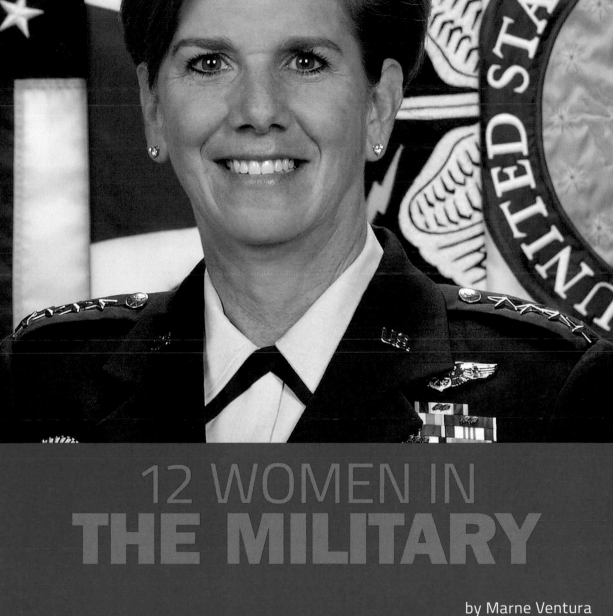

12 WOMEN IN
THE MILITARY

by Marne Ventura

STORY LIBRARY
MORE TO EXPLORE

www.12StoryLibrary.com

12-Story Library is an imprint of Bookstaves.

Photographs ©: US Air Force, cover, 1; 2nd Lt. Austin Lachance/US Army, 4; Michelle Eberhart/US Army, 5; PD, 6-8; Alexeinikolayevichromanov/CC4.0, 9; Ministry of Defence/OGL1.0, 9; Fdutil/CC3.0, 9; chrisdorney/Shutterstock.com, 9; US Air Force, 10; US Air Force, 11; PD, 12; Library of Congress, 13; US Air Force, 14; Senior Master Sgt. Adrian Cadiz/US Military, 15; US Army, 16; Library of Congress, 17; US Army, 18; Staff Sgt. Teddy Wade/US Army, 19; PD, 20; Tijmen Stam/CC2.5, 21; Expert Infantry/CC2.0, 22; CC2.0, 23; PD, 24; Ad Meskens/CC3.0, 25; US Army, 26; Staff Sgt. Christopher Hubenthal/PJF Military Collection/Alamy, 27; PD, 28; US Air Force, 29

ISBN
9781632357809 (hardcover)
9781632358899 (paperback)
9781645820604 (ebook)

Library of Congress Control Number: 2019938619

Printed in the United States of America
September 2019

About the Cover
General Lori J. Robinson, United States Air Force.

Table of Contents

Simone Askew:
West Point Cadet Leader

Simone Askew is the first African American and first woman to be First Captain at West Point, the US Military Academy. She was born in Virginia in 1996. Her mother often took her to football games at the Naval Academy. Askew loved watching the cadets march onto the field. She dreamed that one day she would lead a marching unit.

In high school, Askew was already a leader. She was student body president and captain of the volleyball team. She started the school's Black Student Union. She spent her summers helping in orphanages in the Dominican Republic. After high school, Askew was accepted at West Point. This four-year college trains students called "cadets" to serve in the army. Students must have good grades and high test scores to get in. They must pass a physical fitness test.

Askew excelled at West Point. In 2017, she was chosen to be First Captain of the Core of Cadets. She was 20 years old. She served as liaison between the cadets and heads of the school. Her childhood wish came true. She got to lead the marching unit.

Simone Askew in 2018.

20
Percent of female students at West Point when Simone Askew started there

- Askew's mentor was one of just two African American women to graduate from West Point's first class of women in 1980.
- The school opened an Office of Diversity in 2014 to recruit more women and minorities.
- West Point's class of 2019 included 34 black women, the highest number ever.

Askew leads a class of 2021 new cadets at West Point.

THINK ABOUT IT

As a child, Simone Askew hoped that one day she could lead a marching unit. What is one goal you have for your future? What steps can you take to reach your goal?

Queen Elizabeth I: Good Queen Bess

Queen Elizabeth I was one of England's most powerful rulers. She was born near London in 1533. Her father was King Henry VIII. Her mother was Anne Boleyn. Elizabeth was smart and well educated.

Elizabeth's father died in 1547. Her half-brother, Edward, became king. In 1553, Edward died. Elizabeth's half-sister Mary took the throne. Mary wanted to force all of England to be Catholic instead of Protestant. Many people rebelled. Mary accused Elizabeth of being a Protestant and a traitor. She locked her up for two months. But Mary was unable to prove Elizabeth's guilt.

When Mary died in 1558, Elizabeth became queen. Many people at the time believed that women were inferior to men and unfit to rule. Elizabeth resisted the idea that she needed men to help her govern. Although she had many suitors, she never married. Elizabeth was good at public speaking. She convinced her

A portrait of Queen Elizabeth I circa 1575.

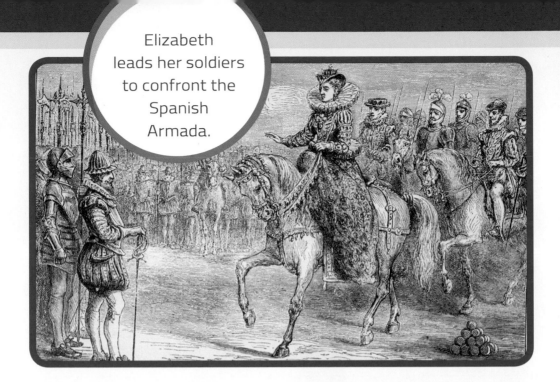

Elizabeth leads her soldiers to confront the Spanish Armada.

people that she was on their side. She gained their love and respect.

Spain was the most powerful country at the time. Its ruler, King Philip, sent a fleet of ships to invade England in 1588. He wanted to remove Elizabeth from the throne. Then he would take over England and make it Catholic. Elizabeth gathered her soldiers on the cliffs above the sea. She joined them on horseback. She thanked her men for their bravery and told them she trusted them. She said she would live or die beside them. Elizabeth's soldiers drove back the Spanish Armada. Historians see this as one of England's greatest wins. They give the Queen credit for leading her men to victory.

130
Number of ships in the Spanish Armada

- King Philip thought his fleet was unbeatable. But the English were ready and waiting.
- The English commanders were Lord Charles Howard and Sir Francis Drake.
- Before he helped crush the Spanish Armada, Drake sailed around the world.

Krystyna Skarbek: Legendary Spy

Krystyna Skarbek in 1945.

mission, she flew to Budapest, Hungary. She posed as a journalist. She skied into Nazi-held Poland. She helped set up supply chains for the resistance, and she helped people escape.

Skarbek gathered information about what the Nazis were doing. It was dangerous work. In 1941, the Gestapo caught her. She bit her tongue to make it bleed. She pretended to have tuberculosis. She fooled the prison doctor. He let her go because he didn't want to catch the disease.

Krystyna Skarbek worked against the Nazis during World War II (1939–1945). She was born Maria Krystyna Janina Skarbek in Poland in 1908. When Hitler invaded Poland in 1939, Britain declared war on Germany. Skarbek went to London to help in the fight. She began to work as a spy. For her first

In 1944, Skarbek parachuted into France. She helped Germans who wanted to defect from the Nazis. The same year, she saved the lives of three other agents. They were about to be killed by the Nazis. She convinced the Nazis that the Allies were about to invade. They let the prisoners go.

3

Number of languages spoken by Krystyna Skarbek

- Skarbek spoke Polish, French, and English.
- She helped the Allies defeat the Nazis in World War II.
- She won three medals for her work as a spy, two from Britain and one from France.

The three medals Skarbek was awarded for her civilian bravery.

FIRST LADY SPY

Skarbek was the first woman to work as a spy for Britain during World War II. Speaking three languages made her very useful. She grew up in Poland, so she knew her way around the area taken over by the Nazis. As a spy, she would ski over secret routes from Hungary to Poland.

4

Elsie Ott: Air Evacuation Pioneer

> Elsie Ott was the first woman to receive the US Air Medal.

Elsie Ott was a flight nurse in the US Army during World War II (1939–1945). She was born in 1913 in New York. After high school, she became a nurse. In 1941, she joined the Army Nurse Corps. The army sent her to India.

The army needed a faster way to get wounded soldiers from battlefields to hospitals. In 1943, they decided to try aircraft instead of ships. Ott was chosen for the first flight. It would travel from

Karachi, India, to Washington, DC. She was told to be ready in 24 hours. She had never flown before.

Ott quickly gathered blankets, sheets, and pillows. But the only medical gear she had was a first aid kit. The plane took off with five patients. They all had different injuries and illnesses. The plane stopped along the way to refuel a few times. It picked up more patients. The plane landed safely in Washington, DC, and the soldiers were taken to Walter Reed Hospital. The trip took less than a week. The same trip by ship would have taken three months.

Ott made notes during the flight. She knew they would help future air evacuations. She listed supplies that should be on hand. Nurses on future flights would need oxygen, wound dressings, coffee, and blankets. Ott suggested that nurses wear pants instead of skirts. Two years later, Ott was the first woman to get a US Air Medal. The Army honored her for her work on the first air evacuation.

1

Number of helpers Elsie Ott had on the first intercontinental air evacuation flight

- Ott had shown that air evacuation could work.
- In the fall of 1943, the army started a training program for flight nurses.
- In 1965, almost 20 years later, Ott was selected to christen the C-9 Nightingale, a new kind of air ambulance.

Harriet Tubman: A Spy for the Union Army

$200
What Harriet Tubman was paid for her work during the war

- She also received a small pension because her husband was a veteran.
- In 2003, Congress gave $11,570 to the Harriet Tubman Home in Auburn, New York.
- This is what the Union Army should have paid Tubman, adjusted for inflation.

Harriet Tubman is best known as an abolitionist and activist. But during the Civil War (1861–1865), she worked for the Union Army. She was the first and only woman to organize a military operation during the war.

She was born Araminta Ross around 1820 in Maryland. Her family was enslaved. She married a free black man, John Tubman, in 1844. She changed her first name to Harriet. But even after her marriage, she was still enslaved. In 1849, Tubman escaped north. She began to work as a conductor for the Underground Railroad. She helped hundreds of blacks escape to Canada.

In 1862, Tubman went to work for the Union Army in South Carolina. She was a cook, a nurse, a scout, and a laundress. She also spied on Confederate soldiers. She found out where their warehouses and ammunition stores were. This helped the Union Army plan their attacks.

In June 1863, Tubman joined a group of Union soldiers on a nighttime raid on Combahee Ferry. Three Union ships sailed up a river into Confederate territory. Tubman told them the safe way to go. More than 700 slaves were freed that night.

HARRIET THE SPY

By the time Harriet Tubman started working for the Union Army, she was already a good spy. She had learned spying skills in her Underground Railroad days. She moved around without drawing attention to herself. She arranged secret meetings. She couldn't read, but she had a very good memory. And she built a spy ring.

Tubman's efforts during the Combahee Ferry Raid freed more than 700 slaves.

13

Lori J. Robinson: Highest-Ranking Woman

Lori Robinson is a US Air Force general. In 2016, she became the highest-ranking woman in US military history. Robinson was born in 1959 in Texas. Her father was an air force fighter pilot. Robinson joined the reserves in college. In 1981, she graduated and began service in the air force. In 1986, she was the first female instructor at the USAF school in Nevada. She earned frequent promotions. By 2014, she was a four-star general. She took command of the Pacific Air Forces.

In 2016, Robinson was given command of NORAD and NORTHCOM. These organizations work together to defend and protect America. This assignment made Robinson the highest-ranking woman in US military history. In the past, top positions in the air force went to fighter pilots. Women were not allowed to fly fighter aircraft until 1993. Robinson was not a fighter pilot. She was an air battle manager.

Robinson's husband was also in the air force. During the first years of their marriage, their family was stationed in Hawaii. The air force wanted to move Robinson's husband to Korea. They wanted to move Robinson to Japan.

Lori Robinson in 2016.

Command being turned over to Robinson, making her the highest-ranking woman in US military history.

The couple did not want to split up their family. So her husband left active duty. He became a commercial pilot. Robinson gives credit to him for helping her succeed in the air force.

THINK ABOUT IT

Robinson became the highest-ranking woman in US military history when she was made commander of NORAD and NORTHCOM. Does her accomplishment help future women in the military? Explain your answer.

37
Lori Robinson's years of military service

- Robinson graduated from college with a degree in English.
- She was the first woman to lead a major military command.
- People who knew her said her abilities set her apart, not her gender.

Cathay Williams: Soldier in Disguise

Cathay Williams was the first black female to enlist in the US Army. But to do that, she had to pretend to be a man. Williams was born in Missouri in 1844. Her mother was enslaved. Her father was free. She worked as a house slave on a plantation. In 1861, Union soldiers took over her area. The soldiers captured the enslaved people, including Williams. She was 17 years old.

Williams worked as an army cook. She did the soldiers' laundry and traveled with them. When the war ended, Williams needed a job. She cut her hair and changed her name to William Cathay. She enlisted in the US Regular Army on November 15, 1866.

Williams became the only known black woman to serve in the army at the time. When she got sick with smallpox, she was put in a hospital. A doctor there discovered that

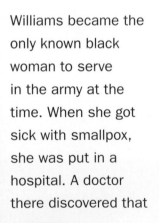

Cathay Williams, posed as a man, in 1866.

"William Cathay" was a woman. She was discharged from the army in 1868. Years later, a reporter interviewed her and wrote about her army service.

Buffalo soldiers of the 25th Infantry.

400+
Number of women who posed as men and served in the Civil War

- When Williams enlisted in the army, she had to pass a medical exam. But it wasn't very thorough.
- Two members of the regiment she joined knew her secret. But they didn't tell anyone.
- Williams's story appeared in the *St. Louis Daily Times* on January 2, 1876.

BUFFALO SOLDIER

After Cathay Williams was discharged from the army, she signed up with a new all-black regiment. It became known as the Buffalo Soldiers. White army leaders commanded the group. Its mission was to protect settlers moving west. They built roads and guarded the US mail. They fought in wars against Native Americans.

17

Ann E. Dunwoody: First US Army Four-Star General

Ann Dunwoody was the first woman to become a four-star general in the US military. She was born in 1953 in Virginia. Dunwoody loved sports and planned to become a coach or PE teacher. When she was a junior in college, the army offered to pay $500 a month to seniors who agreed to serve for two years. She signed up. After she graduated in 1975, she was stationed in Oklahoma.

Dunwoody only planned to stay for two years. She found she liked army life. She signed up for more service. She went to airborne school. It was the first time the army let women follow this career path. She earned two master's degrees while she was serving in the army. In 1992, she became the first woman battalion

ARMY FAMILY

Ann Dunwoody's brother, father, grandfather, and great-grandfather all went to West Point, the US Military Academy. Her older sister became the third female helicopter pilot in the army. Dunwoody says her father was her hero. But her mother inspired her, too. She taught Ann to do the right thing and take care of people.

Dunwoody at her retirement ceremony in 2012.

commander. In 2000, at Fort Bragg, North Carolina, she became the first female general. She received many awards and medals for her service.

In 2008, Dunwoody had been serving for almost 40 years. She became the first American woman to be promoted to four-star general. On the same day, she became head of the army command at Fort Belvoir, Virginia. Dunwoody retired in 2012. In 2015, she published a book about her army career.

69,000
Size of the staff Ann Dunwoody oversaw as a four-star general

- She managed a budget of $60 billion.
- She led many divisions in the United States and abroad.
- She was an expert manager.

Joan of Arc:
French Heroine and Saint

Joan of Arc circa 1428.

During the war, the English and French struggled over who should rule France. The English took over many French towns. In 1427, Charles, a French prince, was in line to be king. But the English would not let him rule.

In 1428, Joan went from her hometown to a French soldiers' camp. She told the captain that she wanted to meet with Charles. He

Joan of Arc was a French peasant girl during the Hundred Years' War (1337–1453). She was born in 1412 in a small French village. At age 12, she believed that God was talking to her. God told her to drive the English out of France.

20

19
Joan of Arc's age when she was killed by the English

- Joan of Arc believed that two saints came to her in visions. They told her what to do.
- The English said Joan broke God's law by dressing as a man and using weapons.
- In 1920, the Catholic Church declared Joan of Arc a saint.

refused. She returned in 1429. She told the captain she could help put the prince back in power. This time, he agreed to let her see Charles. Joan dressed as a man. She rode through enemy territory with six other men. Joan told Charles about her message from God. Charles was skeptical. In the end, he agreed to let her help.

Joan led hundreds of men to a battle at Orléans. The French won. Joan and the men forced the English out of two more towns. Charles was crowned King of France. Joan became a beloved hero to the French people. But in 1430, the English captured Joan. They put her in a prison tower. They accused her of being a witch. In 1431, Joan was put to death.

Grace Hopper: Amazing Grace

Grace Hopper was a computer scientist and navy officer. She was born Grace Murray in New York in 1906. At age 17, she graduated from Vassar College with degrees in math and physics. She went on to earn her master's degree and a PhD in math, both from Yale. She taught math until 1943, then joined the Navy Reserve. This was during World War II (1939–45).

Hopper was assigned to a research project at the Harvard Computation Lab. Its purpose was to use math to solve wartime problems. She worked on the first large-scale automatic calculator. In 1949, Hopper went to work for the company that built one of the first electronic digital computers. She designed a compiler. This is code that takes English words and changes them into numbers computers can understand. Hopper's work led to the development of COBOL. This became the language many businesses used to talk to computers.

In 1966, Hopper took charge of the Navy's use of COBOL. In 1983, she was promoted to commodore in a White House ceremony. Two years later, she became Rear Admiral Hopper.

Grace Hopper in 2011.

While working at Harvard, Hopper found a moth caught inside a switch. She taped the moth in a notebook. Her note said she had found a bug. Today, when something in a computer program doesn't work properly, it's called a bug.

THINK ABOUT IT

Grace Hopper said she was most proud of all the young people she trained. Why do you think she felt this way?

30+
Number of universities that gave Grace Hopper honorary degrees

- Hopper is called the mother of computing.
- She trained many young students to program computers.
- In 1996, the US Navy named a destroyer after her, the *USS Hopper.*

Queen Boudicca: British Folk Hero

Queen Boudicca was a British Celtic queen. She was born around 30 CE. Her husband was king of their tribe. In 43 CE, the Romans took over southern England. The king tried to keep peace with them. He thought they were allies. In his will, he left the rule of the tribe to his daughters and a Roman leader. When he died, the Romans took over the tribe. They mistreated his wife and his daughters.

Boudicca fought back. She formed an army of 100,000 soldiers. She led them in a fight against the Romans. First, they captured one Roman settlement. They set fires and destroyed buildings. They killed many Romans. They moved to a second Roman city and left it in ruins. Then they did the same to a third.

A Roman named Paulinus brought an army to stop them. Before the battle, Boudicca talked to her soldiers. She urged them to be brave and fight for freedom. The Romans trapped

Queen Boudicca, with her daughters, rallying her army of soldiers.

BOUDICCA'S DEATH

Historians are not sure how Boudicca died. Some say she took poison because she didn't want to be captured by the Romans. After her death, a new Roman leader took control. Smaller groups fought the Romans in the years after. None were as big as Boudicca's army. The Romans stayed in control of Britain until 410 CE.

Boudicca's army. When they tried to flee, Roman wagons blocked their path. Boudicca was defeated. Still, she is remembered many centuries later for her strategy, courage, and fierceness in war.

80,000
Number of people killed during Boudicca's rebellion

- Under Roman law, Boudicca could not inherit any of her husband's property.
- A bronze statue of Boudicca in her war chariot stands in London near the Houses of Parliament.
- The statue is a tribute to the queen's fight for freedom and justice.

A statue of Roman General Paulinus, who defeated Boudicca.

Patricia Horoho: Nurse Hero and Army Surgeon General

Patricia Horoho in 2014.

In 1994, she was head nurse on duty at Pope Air Force Base in North Carolina. Two aircraft crashed. Twenty-four people died. Another 100 were hurt. Horoho led the team as they treated the injured. Ten years later, Horoho was working at the Pentagon on the day of the 9/11 terrorist attacks. Rather than leave the building with her coworkers, Horoho stayed at the crash site to help the victims.

Patricia Horoho was the first female Army Surgeon General. She was born in North Carolina in 1960. Her father was an army officer. She studied nursing and then joined the army. She served in the United States and Europe. In 1992, Horoho earned her master's degree in nursing.

In 2008, Horoho became Chief of the US Army Nurse Corps. She was in charge of over 9,000 nurses. In 2010, she was named Deputy Surgeon General of the US Army. In 2011, President Barack Obama chose her to be Surgeon General of the US Army. She was the first woman and the first nurse to hold this position.

2002

Year when the Red Cross named Patricia Horoho a Nurse Hero

- Horoho says the 1994 crash in North Carolina helped prepare her for 9/11.
- When she learned the World Trade Center had been attacked, she knew the Pentagon would be next.
- She is credited with saving dozens of lives at the Pentagon that day.

9/11

On September 11, 2001, Islamic extremists took control of four planes flying over the United States. Two were crashed into the World Trade Center in New York. One flew into the Pentagon, the military headquarters in Washington, DC. The fourth crashed to the ground in Pittsburgh. Almost 3,000 people were killed. Many more were injured.

Horoho discusses combat readiness at a medical conference in 2014.

Out of the Shadows

Rani Lakshmibai circa 1857.

Lakshmibai

Born in 1828, Lakshmibai was the Rani of India's Jhansi state. Rani means "Warrior Queen." After her husband died, the British took control of Jhansi. Lakshmibai led her people in a fight against the British in 1857. Some called her the Indian Joan of Arc. She became an icon for India's struggle for independence from the British.

Zenobia

Born in 240 CE, Zenobia was queen of Palmyra, a Roman colony in what is now Syria. In 267, she became ruler. Zenobia fought fiercely against Roman rule. She conquered Egypt and some of Rome's other lands before she was stopped by the Roman emperor Aurelian.

Aleda Lutz

Born in 1915 in Michigan, Lutz was a World War II army nurse. She spent more hours on the job than any other army nurse. She died in a plane crash at age 28. Historians think she was the first female killed in action in World War II.

Aleda Lutz.

Ruby Bradley

Bradley was born in West Virginia in 1907. She was a heroic Army nurse during World War II. She was serving in the Philippines when the Japanese attacked Pearl Harbor. Three weeks later, she was captured by the Japanese. As a prisoner of war in Manila, she tended to sick and injured prisoners. She smuggled her own food to starving children in the camp. US troops freed her in 1945. Bradley went on to serve in the Korean War.

Glossary

abolitionist
A person who wants to put an end to slavery.

activist
A person who tries to bring about social or political change.

allies
People, countries, or states who have the same goal and are working together.

battalion
A big unit of soldiers.

combat
Active battle in war.

evacuate
To move out of danger.

extremist
A person who supports radical political ideas.

liaison
A person who helps two groups communicate with each other.

mentor
A wise, trusted advisor.

minority
A part of the population that is different in some way and is often treated unfairly.

reserves
A group of military members who are not active but are on call to serve.

skeptical
Doubtful; wanting proof in order to believe.

terrorist
A person or group who uses violent or destructive acts to achieve their goals.

Underground Railroad
A network of people and places that helped enslaved people escape to the North or Canada before the American Civil War.

Conkling, Winifred. *Heroism Begins with Her: Inspiring Stories of Bold, Brave, and Gutsy Women in the U.S. Military.* New York: Harper Collins, 2019.

Mundy, Liza. *Code Girls: The True Story of the American Women Who Secretly Broke Codes in World War II* (Young Readers Edition). New York: Little, Brown and Company, 2018.

Sherman, Jill. *Eyewitness to the Role of Women in World War II.* Eyewitness to World War II. Mankato, MN: Childs World, 2016.

Index

About the Author

Marne Ventura has written over 100 books for children. A former elementary school teacher, she holds a master's degree in education from the University of California. Marne and her husband live on the central coast of California.

READ MORE FROM 12-STORY LIBRARY

Every 12-Story Library Book is available in many fomats. For more information, visit **12StoryLibrary.com**